A Yorkshire Tragedy by Thomas Middleton

In 1608, A Yorkshire Tragedy appeared in quarto. It was one of four short plays performed at the Globe; the other three are now lost. Originally attributed to Shakespeare the bulk of it is now firmly under the authorship of Middleton.

Thomas Middleton was born in London in April 1580 and baptised on 18th April.

Middleton was aged only five when his father died. His mother remarried but this unfortunately fell apart into a fifteen year legal dispute regarding the inheritance due Thomas and his younger sister.

By the time he left Oxford, at the turn of the Century, Middleton had and published Microcynicon: Six Snarling Satirese which was denounced by the Archbishop of Canterbury and publicly burned.

In the early years of the 17th century, Middleton wrote topical pamphlets. One – Penniless Parliament of Threadbare Poets was reprinted several times and the subject of a parliamentary inquiry.

These early years writing plays continued to attract controversy. His writing partnership with Thomas Dekker brought him into conflict with Ben Jonson and George Chapman in the so-called War of the Theatres.

His finest work with Dekker was undoubtedly The Roaring Girl, a biography of the notorious Mary Frith.

In the 1610s, Middleton began another playwriting partnership, this time with the actor William Rowley, producing another slew of plays including Wit at Several Weapons and A Fair Quarrel.

The ever adaptable Middleton seemed at ease working with others or by himself. His solo writing credits include the comic masterpiece, A Chaste Maid in Cheapside, in 1613.

In 1620 he was officially appointed as chronologer of the City of London, a post he held until his death.

The 1620s saw the production of his and Rowley's tragedy, and continual favourite, The Changeling, and of several other tragicomedies.

However in 1624, he reached a peak of notoriety when his dramatic allegory A Game at Chess was staged by the King's Men. Though Middleton's approach was strongly patriotic, the Privy Council silenced the play after only nine performances at the Globe theatre, having received a complaint from the Spanish ambassador.

What happened next is a mystery. It is the last play recorded as having being written by Middleton.

Thomas Middleton died at his home at Newington Butts in Southwark in the summer of 1627, and was buried on July 4th, in St Mary's churchyard which today survives as a public park in Elephant and Castle.

Index of Contents

Dramatis Personae
(in order of appearance)
OLIVER }
RALPH   } serving-men of a house in Yorkshire
SAM   }
A Boy
The WIFE
The HUSBAND
Four GENTLEMEN
A SERVANT
The MASTER of a College
The SON
A MAID
A LUSTY SERVANT
KNIGHT, a magistrate
Officers

SCENE I. A House in Yorkshire

Enter **OLIVER** and **RALPH**, two serving-men.

OLIVER
Sirrah Ralph, my young mistress is in such a pitiful, passionate humour for the long absence of her love.

RALPH
Why, can you blame her? Why, apples hanging longer on the tree then when they are ripe make so many fallings. Viz, mad wenches, because they are not gathered in time, are fain to drop of themselves, and then 'tis common, you know, for every man to take 'em up.

OLIVER
Mass, thou sayest true, 'tis common indeed. But, sirrah, is neither our young master returned, nor our fellow Sam come from London?

RALPH
Neither of either, as the puritan bawd says.

[Noise within]

'Slid, I hear Sam; Sam's come, here's tarry. Come, i'faith, now my nose itches for news.

OLIVER
And so does mine elbow.

SAM [Calls within]
Where are you there?

[Enter **SAM** and a **BOY**.

Boy, look you walk my horse with discretion; I have rid him simply. I warrant his skin sticks to his back with very heat; if 'a should catch cold and get the cough of the lungs, I were well served, were I not?

[Exit **BOY**.

What, Ralph and Oliver!

AMBO
Honest fellow Sam, welcome, i'faith! What tricks hast thou brought from London?

[**SAM** is furnished with things from London which he now presents.

SAM
You see I am hang'd after the truest fashion: three hats, and two glasses bobbling upon 'em, two rebato wires upon my breast, a cap-case by my side, a brush at my back, an almanac in my pocket, and three ballads in my codpiece. Nay, I am the true picture of a common serving-man.

OLIVER
I'll swear thou art. Thou mayest set up when thou wilt. There's many a one begins with less, I can tell thee, that proves a rich man ere he dies. But what's the news from London, Sam?

RALPH
Ay, that's well fed. What's the news from London, sirrah? My young mistress keeps such a puling for her love.

SAM
Why? The more fool she, ay, the more ninnyhammer she.

OLIVER

Why, Sam, why?

SAM
Why, he's married to another long ago.

AMBO
I'faith, ye jest.

SAM
Why, did you not know that till now? Why, he's married, beats his wife, and has two or three children by her: for you must note that any woman bears the more when she is beaten.

RALPH
Ay, that's true, for she bears the blows.

OLIVER
Sirrah Sam, I would not for two years' wages my young mistress knew so much. She'd run upon the left hand of her wit, and ne'er be her own woman again.

SAM
And I think she was blest in her cradle, that he never came in her bed. Why, he has consumed all, pawned his lands, and made his university brother stand in wax for him. There's a fine phrase for a scrivener. Puh, he owes more than his skin's worth.

OLIVER
Is't possible?

SAM
Nay, I'll tell you moreover he calls his wife whore as familiarly as one would call Moll and Doll, and his children bastards as naturally as can be. But what have we here?

[Pulls out two poting-sticks

I thought 'twas somewhat pulled down my breeches: I quite forget my two poting-sticks. These came from London; now anything is good here that came from London.

OLIVER
Ay, farfetched, you know.

SAM
But speak in your conscience, i'faith: have not we as good poting-sticks i' th' country as need to be put i' th' fire? The mind of a thing is all, the mind of a thing is all. And as thou saidst e'en now, farfetched is the best thing for ladies.

OLIVER
Ay, and for waiting gentlewomen, too.

SAM

But Ralph, what, is our beer sour, this thunder?

OLIVER
No, no, it holds countenance yet.

SAM
Why then, follow me. I'll teach you the finest humour to be drunk it; I learn'd it at London last week.

AMBO
Ay, faith, let's hear it, let's hear it.

SAM
The bravest humour, 'twould do a man good to be drunk in't. They call it knighting in London, when they drink upon their knees.

AMBO
Faith, that's excellent!

SAM
Come, follow me. I'll give you all the degrees on't in order.

Exeunt.

SCENE II. Outside the Husband's House, Near Yorkshire

Enter **WIFE**.

WIFE
What will become of us? All will away.
My husband never ceases in expense,
Both to consume his credit and his house.
And 'tis set down by Heaven's just decree,
That riot's child must needs be beggary.
Are these the virtues that his youth did promise:
Dice, and voluptuous meetings, midnight revels,
Taking his bed with surfeits, ill-beseeming
The ancient honour of his house and name?
And this not all: but that which kills me most,
When he recounts his losses and false fortunes,
The weakness of his state so much dejected,
Not as a man repentant, but half mad.
His fortunes cannot answer his expense.
He sits and sullenly locks up his arms,
Forgetting Heaven looks downward, which makes him
Appear so dreadful, that he frights my heart;
Walks heavily, as if his soul were on earth,

Not penitent for those his sins are past,
But vex'd his money cannot make them last:
A fearful melancholy, ungodly sorrow.
Oh, yonder he comes; now in despite of ills,
I'll speak to him, and I will hear him speak,
And do my best to drive it from his heart.

[Enter **HUSBAND**.

HUSBAND
Pox o' th' last throw, it made
Five hundred angels vanish from my sight!
I'm damn'd, I'm damn'd: the angels have forsook me!
Nay, 'tis certainly true, for he that has no coin
Is damn'd in this world: he's gone, he's gone.

WIFE
Dear husband.

HUSBAND
Oh, most punishment of all, I have a wife!

WIFE
I do entreat you as you love your soul,
Tell me the cause of this your discontent.

HUSBAND
A vengeance strip thee naked, thou art cause,
Effect, quality, property, thou, thou, thou!

[Exit **HUSBAND**.

WIFE
Bad turn'd to worse? Both beggary of the soul,
As of the body; and so much unlike
Himself at first, as if some vexed spirit
Had got his form upon him.

[Enter **HUSBAND**.

[Aside] He comes again.
He says I am the cause: I never yet
Spoke less than words of duty and of love.

HUSBAND [Aside]
If marriage be honourable, then cuckolds are honourable, for they cannot be made without marriage.
Fool! What meant I to marry to get beggars? Now must my eldest son be a knave or nothing. He cannot
live upon the soil, for he will have no land to maintain him: that mortgage sits like a snaffle upon mine

inheritance, and makes me chew upon iron. My second son must be a promoter, and my third a thief, or an underputter, a slave pander. Oh beggary, beggary, to what base uses does thou put a man!
I think the devil scorns to be a bawd:
He bears himself more proudly, has more care on's credit.
Base, slavish, abject, filthy poverty!

WIFE
Good sir, by all our vows I do beseech you,
Show me the true cause of your discontent.

HUSBAND
Money, money, money, and thou must supply me!

WIFE
Alas, I am the least cause of your discontent;
Yet what is mine, either in rings or jewels,
Use to your own desire. But I beseech you,
As y'are a gentleman by many bloods,
Though I myself be out of your respect,
Think on the state of these three lovely boys
You have been father to.

HUSBAND
Puh! Bastards, bastards,
Bastards, begot in tricks, begot in tricks!

WIFE
Heaven knows how those words wrong me! But I may
Endure these griefs among a thousand more.
Oh, call to mind your lands already mortgaged,
Yourself wound into debts, your hopeful brother
At the university in bonds for you,
Like to be seiz'd upon. And—

HUSBAND
Ha' done, thou harlot,
Whom though for fashion sake I married,
I never could abide? Thinkst thou thy words
Shall kill my pleasures? Fall off to thy friends,
Thou and thy bastards beg: I will not bate
A whit in humour.—Midnight, still I love you
And revel in your company. Curb'd in,
Shall it be said in all societies
That I broke custom, that I flagg'd in money?
No, those thy jewels I will play as freely
As when my state was fullest.

WIFE

Be it so.

HUSBAND
Nay, I protest, and take that for an earnest!

[Spurns her.

I will forever hold thee in contempt,
And never touch the sheets that cover thee;
But be divorc'd in bed till thou consent
Thy dowry shall be sold to give new life
Unto those pleasures which I most affect.

WIFE
Sir, do but turn a gentle eye on me,
And what the law shall give me leave to do
You shall command.

HUSBAND
Look it be done.

[Holding his hands in his pockets.

Shall I want dust and like a slave
Wear nothing in my pockets but my hands
To fill them up with nails?
Oh, much against my blood! Let it be done;
I was never made to be a looker on.
A bawd to dice? I'll shake the drabs myself
And make 'em yield. I say, look it be done!

WIFE
I take my leave; it shall.

HUSBAND
Speedily, speedily!

[Exit **WIFE**.

I hate the very hour I chose a wife, a trouble, trouble, three children like three evils hang upon me! Fie, fie, fie, strumpet and bastards, strumpet and bastards!

[Enter three **GENTLEMEN** hearing him.

FIRST GENTLEMAN
Still do those loathsome thoughts jar on your tongue,
Yourself to stain the honour of your wife,
Nobly descended. Those whom men call mad

Endanger others, but he's more than mad
That wounds himself, whose own words do proclaim
Scandals unjust, to foil his better name:
It is not fit. I pray, forsake it.

SECOND GENTLEMAN
Good sir, let modesty reprove you.

THIRD GENTLEMAN
Let honest kindness sway so much with you.

HUSBAND
God-den, I thank you, sir. How do you? Adieu. I'm glad to see you. Farewell.

[Exit **GENTLEMEN**.

Instructions! Admonitions!

[Enter **SERVANT**.

How now, sirrah, what would you?

SERVANT
Only to certify to you, sir, that my mistress was met by the way, by these who were sent for her to London by her honourable uncle, your worship's late guardian.

HUSBAND
So, sir, then she is gone and so may you be.
But let her look that the thing be done she wots of,
Or Hell will stand more pleasant than her house at home.

[Exit **SERVANT**.

[Enter a Fourth **GENTLEMAN**.

FOURTH GENTLEMAN
Well or ill met, I care not.

HUSBAND
No, nor I.

FOURTH GENTLEMAN
I am come with confidence to chide you.

HUSBAND
Who, me? Chide me? Do't finely, then: let it not move me, for if thou chid'st me, angry I shall strike.

FOURTH GENTLEMAN

Strike thine own follies, for it is they
Deserve to be well beaten. We are now in private;
There's none but thou and I. Thou'rt fond and peevish,
An unclean rioter, thy lands and credit
Lie now both sick of a consumption.
I am sorry for thee: that man spends with shame
That with his riches does consume his name,
And such art thou.

HUSBAND
Peace!

FOURTH GENTLEMAN
No, thou shalt hear me further.
Thy father's and forefathers' worthy honours,
Which were our country's monuments, our grace,
Follies in thee begin now to deface.
The springtime of thy youth did fairly promise
Such a most fruitful summer to thy friends,
It scarce can enter into men's beliefs
Such dearth should hang on thee. We that see it
Are sorry to believe it. In thy change
This voice into all places will be hurl'd:
Thou and the devil have deceived the world.

HUSBAND
I'll not endure thee!

FOURTH GENTLEMAN
But of all the worst:
Thy virtuous wife, right honourably allied,
Thou hast proclaimed a strumpet.

HUSBAND
Nay, then, I know thee:
Thou art her champion, thou, her private friend,
The party you wot on.

FOURTH GENTLEMAN
Oh, ignoble thought!
I am past my patient blood. Shall I stand idle
And see my reputation touch'd to death?

HUSBAND
'T'as gall'd you this, has it?

FOURTH GENTLEMAN
No, monster, I will prove

My thoughts did only tend to virtuous love.

HUSBAND
Love of her virtues? There it goes!

FOURTH GENTLEMAN
Base spirit,
To lay thy hate upon the fruitful honour
Of thine own bed!

[They draw their swords and fight, and the **HUSBAND** is hurt.

HUSBAND
Oh!

FOURTH GENTLEMAN
Woult thou yield it yet?

HUSBAND
Sir, sir, I have not done with you.

GENTLEMAN
I hope, nor ne'er shall do.

[Fight again.

HUSBAND
Have you got tricks?
Are you in cunning with me?

FOURTH GENTLEMAN
No, plain and right.
He needs no cunning that for truth doth fight.

[**HUSBAND** is wounded and falls down.

HUSBAND
Hard fortune, am I leveled with the ground?

FOURTH GENTLEMAN
Now, sir, you lie at mercy.

HUSBAND
Ay, you slave!

FOURTH GENTLEMAN
Alas, that hate should bring us to our grave!
You see my sword's not thirsty for your life.

I am sorrier for your wound than yourself.
Y'are of a virtuous house: show virtuous deeds;
'Tis not your honour, 'tis your folly bleeds.
Much good has been expected in your life:
Cancel not all men's hopes. You have a wife
Kind and obedient: heap not wrongful shame
On her, your posterity. Let only sin be sore,
And by this fall, rise never to fall more.
And so I leave you.

[Exit **GENTLEMAN**.

HUSBAND
Has the dog left me then
After his tooth hath left me? Oh, my heart
Would fain leap after him; revenge, I say!
I'm mad to be reveng'd! My strumpet wife,
It is thy quarrel that rips thus my flesh,
And makes my breast spit blood! But thou shalt bleed.
Vanquish'd? Got down? Unable e'en to speak?
Surely 'tis want of money makes men weak.
Ay, 'twas that o'erthrew me; I'd ne'er been down else.

[Exit.

SCENE III. The Husband's House, A Room Above

Enter **WIFE** in a riding suit with a serving-man.

SERVANT
Faith, mistress, if it might not be presumption
In me to tell you so, for his excuse,
You had small reason, knowing his abuse.

WIFE
I grant I had, but alas,
Why should our faults at home be spread abroad?
'Tis grief enough within doors. At first sight
Mine uncle could run o'er his prodigal life
As perfectly as if his serious eye
Had numbered all his follies,
Knew of his mortgag'd lands, his friends in bonds,
Himself withered with debts; and in that minute
Had I added his usage and unkindness,
'Twould have confounded every thought of good:
Where now, fathering his riots on his youth,

Which time and tame experience will shake off,
Guessing his kindness to me—as I smoothed him
With all the skill I had, though his deserts
Are in form uglier than an unshap'd bear—
He's ready to prefer him to some office
And place at court, a good and sure relief
To all his stooping fortunes; 'twill be a means, I hope,
To make new league between us, and redeem
His virtues with his lands.

SERVANT
I should think so, mistress. If he should not now be kind to you and love you, and cherish you up, I should think the devil himself kept open house in him.

WIFE
I doubt not but he will now. Prithee, leave me; I think I hear him coming.

SERVANT
I am gone.

[Exit.

WIFE
By this good means I shall preserve my lands,
And free my husband out of usurers' hands:
Now there is no need of sale. My uncle's kind;
I hope, if aught, this will content his mind.
Here comes my husband.

[Enter **HUSBAND**.

HUSBAND
Now, are you come? Where's the money, let's see the money. Is the rubbish sold, those wiseacres, your lands? Why, when! The money, where is't? Pour't down, down with it, down with it! I say, pour't o' th' ground; let's see't, let's see't!

WIFE
Good sir, keep but in patience, and I hope
My words shall like you well. I bring you better
Comfort than the sale of my dowry.

HUSBAND
Hah? What's that?

WIFE
Pray, do not fright me, sir, but vouchsafe me hearing. My uncle, glad of your kindness to me and mild usage—
For so I made it to him—has in pity

Of your declining fortunes, provided
A place for you at court of worth and credit,
Which so much overjoyed me.

HUSBAND
Out on thee, filth!
Over and overjoyed, when I'm in torments?

[Spurns her.

Thou politic whore, subtler than nine devils, was this thy journey to nuncle, to set down the history of me, of my state and fortunes? Shall I that dedicated myself to pleasure be now confin'd in service to crouch and stand like an old man i' th' hams, my hat off, I that never could abide to uncover my head i' th' church, base slut? This fruit bears thy complaints!

WIFE
Oh, Heaven knows
That my complaints were praises, and best words
Of you, and your estate: only my friends
Knew of your mortgag'd lands, and were possess'd
Of every accident before I came.
If thou suspect it but a plot in me
To keep my dowry, or for mine own good
Or my poor children's—though it suits a mother
To show a natural care in their reliefs,
Yet I'll forget myself to calm your blood—
Consume it, as your pleasure counsels you;
And all I wish, e'en clemency affords,
Give me but comely looks and modest words.

HUSBAND
Money, whore, money, or I'll—

[The **HUSBAND** draws his dagger.

[Enter a **SERVANT** very hastily. The **HUSBAND** speaks to his man.

What the devil? How now? Thy hasty news?

[**SERVANT** in a fear.

SERVANT
May it please you, sir.

HUSBAND
What? May I not look upon my dagger? Speak, villain, or I will execute the point on thee: quick, short!

SERVANT

Why, sir, a gentleman from the university stays below to speak with you.

HUSBAND
From the university? So, university:
That long word runs through me.

[Exeunt **HUSBAND** and **SERVANT**. **WIFE** alone.

WIFE
Was ever wife so wretchedly beset?
Had not this news stepp'd in between, the point
Had offered violence to my breast.
That which some women call great misery
Would show but little here, would scarce be seen
Amongst my miseries. I may compare
For wretched fortunes with all wives that are;
Nothing will please him, until all be nothing.
He calls it slavery to be prefer'd;
A place of credit, a base servitude.
What shall become of me, and my poor children,
Two here, and one at nurse, my pretty beggars?
I see how ruin with a palsy hand
Begins to shake the ancient feet to dust;
The heavy weight of sorrow draws my lids
Over my dankish eyes, I can scarce see.
Thus grief will last; it wakes and sleeps with me.

SCENE IV. The Husband's House

Enter the **HUSBAND** with the **MASTER** of the College.

HUSBAND
Pray you draw near, sir, y'are exceeding welcome.

MASTER
That's my doubt, I fear; I come not to be welcome.

HUSBAND
Yes, howsoever.

MASTER
'Tis not my fashion, sir, to dwell in long circumstance, but to be plain and effectual, therefore to the purpose. The cause of my setting forth was piteous and lamentable. That hopeful young gentleman, your brother, whose virtues we all love dearly through your default and unnatural negligence, lies in bond executed for your debt, a prisoner, all his studies amazed, his hope strook dead, and the pride of his youth muffled in these dark clouds of oppression.

HUSBAND
Hum, um, um.

MASTER
Oh, you have killed the towardest hope of all our university! Wherefore without repentance and amends, expect ponderous and sudden judgments to fall grievously upon you. Your brother, a man who profited in his divine employments, might have made ten thousand souls fit for Heaven, now by your careless courses cast in prison which you must answer for; and assure your spirit it will come home at length.

HUSBAND
Oh, God, oh.

MASTER
Wifmen think ill of you, others speak ill of you, no man loves you; nay, even those whom honesty condemns, condemn you. And take this from the virtuous affection I bear your brother, never look for prosperous hour, good thought, quiet sleeps, contented walks, nor anything that makes man perfect till you redeem him. What is your answer? How will you bestow him? Upon desperate misery, or better hopes? I suffer till I hear your answer.

HUSBAND
Sir, you have much wrought with me. I feel you in my soul; you are your arts' master. I never had sense till now; your syllables have cleft me. Both for your words and pains I thank you: I cannot but acknowledge grievous wrongs done to my brother, mighty, mighty, mighty wrongs. Within there?

[Enter a **SERVING-MAN**.

SERVANT
Sir.

HUSBAND
Fill me a bowl of wine.

[Exit **SERVANT** for wine.

Alas, poor brother,
Bruis'd with an execution for my sake!

MASTER
A bruise indeed makes many a mortal
Sore till the grave cure 'em.

[Enter **SERVANT** with wine.

HUSBAND
Sir, I begin to you; y'have chid your welcome.

MASTER
I could have wish'd it better for your sake.
I pledge you, sir, to the kind man in prison.

HUSBAND
Let it be so.

[Drink both.

Now, sir, if you please to spend but a few minutes in a walk about my grounds below, my man shall attend you. I doubt not but by that time to be furnish'd of a sufficient answer, and therein my brother fully satisfied.

MASTER
Good sir, in that the angels would be pleas'd, and the world's murmurs calm'd, and I should say I set forth then upon a lucky day.

[Exit **MASTER** with **SERVANT**.

HUSBAND
Oh thou confused man, thy pleasant sins have undone thee, thy damnation has beggar'd thee! That Heaven should say we must not sin, and yet made women, gives our senses way to find pleasure, which being found, confounds us. Why should we know those things so much misuse us? Oh, would virtue had been forbidden, we should then have proved all virtuous, for 'tis our blood to love what we are forbidden! Had not drunkenness been forbidden, what man would have been fool to a beast, and zany to a swine to show tricks in the mire? What is there in three dice to make a man draw thrice three thousand acres into the compass of a round little table, and with the gentleman's palsy in the hand, shake out his posterity? Thieves or beggars; 'tis done, I ha' done't, i'faith! Terrible, horrible misery! How well was I left, very well, very well! My lands showed like a full moon about me, but now the moon's i' th' last quarter, waning, waning. And I am mad to think that moon was mine: mine and my father's, and my forefathers', generations, generations. Down goes the house of us, down, down, it sinks. Now is the name a beggar, begs in me that name which hundreds of years has made this shire famous: in me, and my posterity runs out. In my seed five are made miserable besides myself. My riot is now my brother's jailer, my wife's sighing, my three boys' penury, and mine own confusion.

[Tears his hair.

Why sit my hairs upon my cursed head?
Will not this poison scatter them? Oh, my brother's
In execution among devils
That stretch him and make him give. And I in want,
Not able for to live, nor to redeem him.
Divines and dying men may talk of Hell,
But in my heart her several torments dwell.
Slavery and misery! Who in this case
Would not take up money upon his soul,
Pawn his salvation, live at interest?
I that did ever in abundance dwell,

For me to want, exceeds the throes of Hell!

[Enters his little **SON** with a top and a scourge.

SON
What ails you, father? Are you not well? I cannot scourge my top as long as you stand so: you take up all the room with your wide legs. Puh, you cannot make me afear'd with this; I fear no vizards, nor bugbears.

HUSBAND takes up the **CHILD** by the skirts of his long coat in one hand and draws his dagger with th' other.

HUSBAND
Up, sir, for here thou hast no inheritance left!

SON
Oh, what will you do, father? I am your white boy.

HUSBAND
Thou shalt be my red boy; take that!

[Strikes him.

SON
Oh, you hurt me, father!

HUSBAND
My eldest beggar, thou shalt not live to ask an usurer bread, to cry at a great man's gate, or follow "Good your honour!" by a coach; no, nor your brother. 'Tis charity to brain you.

SON
How shall I learn now my head's broke?

[The **HUSBAND** stabs him.

HUSBAND
Bleed, bleed, rather than beg, beg;
Be not thy name's disgrace.
Spurn thou thy fortunes first if they be base.
Come view thy second brother. Fates,
My children's blood shall spin into your faces!
You shall see
How confidently we scorn beggary!

[Exit with his **SON**.

SCENE V. The Husband's House, The Room Above

Enter a **MAID** with a **CHILD** in her arms, the **MOTHER** [**WIFE**] by her asleep.

MAID
Sleep, sweet babe: sorrow makes thy mother sleep.
It bodes small good when Heaven falls so deep.
Hush, pretty boy, thy hopes might have been better;
'Tis lost at dice what ancient honours won,
Hard when the father plays away the son;
Nothing but misery serves in this house.
Ruin and desolation, oh!

[Enter **HUSBAND** with the **BOY** bleeding.

HUSBAND
Whore, give me that boy!

[Strives with her for the **CHILD**.

MAID
Oh, help, help! Out, alas! Murder, murder!

HUSBAND
Are you gossiping, prating, sturdy quean?
I'll break your clamour with your neck downstairs:
Tumble, tumble, headlong!

[Throws her down.

So, the surest way to charm a woman's tongue
Is break her neck: a politician did it.

SON
Mother, mother, I am kill'd, mother!

[The **WIFE** wakes.

WIFE
Ha, who's that cried? Oh me, my children!
Both, both, both bloody, bloody!

[Catches up the youngest.

HUSBAND
Strumpet, let go the boy, let go the beggar!

WIFE

Oh, my sweet husband!

HUSBAND
Filth, harlot!

WIFE
Oh, what will you do, dear husband?

HUSBAND
Give me the bastard!

WIFE
Your own sweet boy!

HUSBAND
There are too many beggars!

WIFE
Good my husband—

HUSBAND
Dost thou prevent me still?

[Stabs at the **CHILD** in her arms.

WIFE
Oh God!

HUSBAND
Have at his heart!

WIFE
Oh, my dear boy!

[The **HUSBAND** gets it from her.

HUSBAND
Brat, thou shalt not live to shame thy house!

WIFE
Oh Heaven!

[She's hurt and sinks down.

HUSBAND
And perish now, be gone!
There's whores enow, and want would make thee one!

[Enter a **LUSTY SERVANT**

LUSTY SERVANT
Oh, sir, what deeds are these?

HUSBAND
Base slave, my vassal,
Comest thou between my fury to question me?

LUSTY SERVANT
Were you the devil, I would hold you, sir.

HUSBAND
Hold me? Presumption, I'll undo thee for't!

LUSTY SERVANT
'Sblood, you have undone us all, sir.

HUSBAND
Tug at thy master?

LUSTY SERVANT
Tug at a monster!

HUSBAND
Have I no power? Shall my slave fetter me?

[The **HUSBSAND** wrestles with the **SERVANT**.

LUSTY SERVANT
Nay then, the devil wrastles! I am thrown!

HUSBAND
Oh, villain, now I'll tug thee, now I'll tear thee!

[Overcomes him and kicks him with his spurs.

Set quick spurs to my vassal, bruise him, trample him!
So, I think thou wilt not follow me in haste.
My horse stands ready saddled; away, away!
Now to my brat at nurse, my sucking beggar:
Fates, I'll not leave you one to trample on!

SCENE VI. The Husband's House, The Room Below

The **HUSBAND** enters and the **MASTER** meets him.

MASTER
How is't with you, sir?
Methinks you look of a distracted colour.

HUSBAND
Who, I, sir? 'Tis but your fancy.
Please you walk in, sir, and I'll soon resolve you.
I want one small part to make up the sum,
And then my brother shall rest satisfied.

MASTER
I shall be glad to see it, sir. I'll attend you.

[Exeunt.

SCENE VII. The Husband's House, The Room Above

LUSTY SERVANT
Oh, I am scarce able to heave up myself:
H'as so bruis'd me with his devilish weight,
And torn my flesh with his blood-hasty spur.
A man before of easy constitution
Till now, Hell's power supplied to his soul's wrong.
Oh, how damnation can make weak men strong!

[Enter **MASTER** and two **SERVANTS**.

Oh, the most piteous deed, sir, since you came!

MASTER
A deadly greeting! Has he summ'd up this
To satisfy his brother? Here's another:
And by the bleeding infants, the dead mother!

WIFE
Oh, oh!

MASTER
Surgeons, surgeons! She recovers life!
One of his men all faint and bloodied!

LUSTY SERVANT
Follow; our murderous master has took horse
To kill his child at nurse! Oh, follow quickly!

MASTER
I am the readiest; it shall be my charge
To raise the town upon him!

LUSTY SERVANT
Good sir, do follow him.

[Exeunt **MASTER** and **SERVANTS**.

WIFE
Oh, my children!

LUSTY SERVANT
How is it with my most afflicted mistress?

WIFE
Why do I now recover? Why half live?
To see my children bleed before mine eyes,
A sight able to kill a mother's breast
Without an executioner! What, art thou mangled, too?

LUSTY SERVANT
I, thinking to prevent what his quick mischiefs
Had so soon acted, came and rush'd upon him.
We struggled, but a fouler strength than his
O'erthrew me with his arms; then did he bruise me
And rent my flesh, and robb'd me of my hair
Like a man mad in execution,
Made me unfit to rise and follow him.

WIFE
What is it has beguil'd him of all grace
And stole away humanity from his breast,
To slay his children, purpos'd to kill his wife,
And spoil his servants?

[Enter two **SERVANTS**.

AMBO
Please you, leave this most accursed place;
A surgeon waits within.

WIFE
Willing to leave it.
'Tis guilty of sweet blood, innocent blood.
Murder has took this chamber with full hands,
And will ne'er out as long as the house stands.

[Exeunt.

Enter **HUSBAND** as being thrown off his horse, and falls.

HUSBAND
Oh, stumbling jade, the spavin overtake thee,
The fifty diseases stop thee!
Oh, I am sorely bruis'd! Plague founder thee!
Thou runn'st at ease and pleasure, heart, of chance
To throw me now with a flight o' th' town,
In such plain even ground!
'Sfoot, a man may dice upon't,
And throw away the meadows, filthy beast!

CRY WITHIN
Follow, follow, follow!

HUSBAND
Ha? I hear sounds of men, like hew and cry.
Up, up, and struggle to thy horse! Make on!
Dispatch that little beggar and all's done!

CRY WITHIN
Here, this way, this way!

HUSBAND
At my back? Oh,
What fate have I! My limbs deny me go.
My will is bated; beggary claims a part.
Oh, could I here reach to the infant's heart!

[Enter **MASTER** of the College, three **GENTLEMEN**, and **OTHERS** with halberds. They find him.

ALL
Here, here, yonder, yonder!

MASTER
Unnatural, flinty, more than barbarous:
The Scythians in their marble-hearted fates
Could not have acted more remorseless deeds
In their relentless natures than these of thine!
Was this the answer I long waited on,
The satisfaction of thy prisoned brother?

HUSBAND
Why, he can have no more on's than our skins,
And some of 'em want but fleaing.

FIRST GENTLEMAN
Great sins have made him impudent.

MASTER
H'as shed so much blood that he cannot blush.

SECOND GENTLEMAN
Away with him; bear him along to the justice!
A gentleman of worship dwells at hand;
There shall his deeds be blaz'd.

HUSBAND
Why, all the better.
My glory 'tis to have my action known.
I grieve for nothing, but I miss'd of one.

MASTER
There's little of a father in that grief.
Bear him away.

[Exeunt.

SCENE IX. The Knight's House

Enters a **KNIGHT** with two or three **GENTLEMEN**.

KNIGHT
Endangered so his wife? Murdered his children?

FOURTH GENTLEMAN
So the cry comes.

KNIGHT
I am sorry I e'er knew him,
That ever he took life and natural being
From such an honoured stock and fair descent
Till this black minute without stain or blemish.

FOURTH GENTLEMAN
Here come the men.

[Enter the **MASTER** of the College and the rest, with the **HUSBAND** prisoner.

KNIGHT
The serpent of his house?
I'm sorry for this time that I am in place of justice.

MASTER
Please you, sir.

KNIGHT
Do not repeat it twice: I know too much.
Would it had ne'er been thought on.
Sir, I bleed for you.

FOURTH GENTLEMAN
Your father's sorrows are alive in men:
What made you show such monstrous cruelty?

HUSBAND
In a word, sir,
I have consum'd all, play'd away Longacre,
And I thought it the charitablest deed I could do
To cozen beggary, and knock my house o' th' head.

KNIGHT
Oh, in a cooler blood you will repent it!

HUSBAND
I repent now, that one's left unkill'd,
My brat at nurse. Oh, I would full fain have wean'd him!

KNIGHT
Well, I do not think but in tomorrow's judgment
The terror will sit closer to your soul
When the dread thought of death remembers you;
To further which, take this sad voice from me:
Never was act play'd more unnaturally.

HUSBAND
I thank you, sir.

KNIGHT
Go, lead him to the jail,
Where justice claims all; there must pity fail.

HUSBAND
Come, come, away with me.

[Exit the **HUSBAND** as prisoner.

MASTER
Sir, you deserve the worship of your place;
Would all did so: in you the law is grace.

KNIGHT
It is my wish it should be so. Ruinous man,
The desolation of his house, the blot
Upon his predecessors' honour'd name:
That man is nearest shame that is past shame.

[Exeunt.

SCENE X. Outside the Husband's House

Enter **HUSBAND** with the **OFFICERS**, the **MASTER** and **GENTLEMEN** as going by his house.

HUSBAND
I am right against my house, seat of my ancestors.
I hear my wife's alive, but much endangered:
Let me entreat to speak with her before
The prison gripe me.

[Enter his **WIFE** brought in a chair.

FIRST GENTLEMAN
See, here she comes of herself.

WIFE
Oh, my sweet husband, my dear distressed husband,
Now in the hands of unrelenting laws,
My greatest sorrow, my extremest bleeding,
Now my soul bleeds!

HUSBAND
How now? Kind to me? Did I not wound thee, left thee for dead?

WIFE
Tut, far greater wounds did my breast feel:
Unkindness strikes a deeper wound than steel.
You have been still unkind to me.

HUSBAND
Faith, and so I think I have.
I did my murthers roughly out of hand,
Desperate and sudden, but thou hast devis'd

A fine way now to kill me; thou hast given mine eyes
Seven wounds a piece. Now glides the devil from
Me, departs at every joint, heaves up my nails!
Oh, catch him! New torments that were ne'er invented!
Bind him one thousand more, you blessed angels,
In that pit bottomless! Let him not rise
To make men act unnatural tragedies,
To spread into a father, and in fury,
Make him his children's executioners,
Murder his wife, his servants, and who not!
For that man's dark where Heaven is quite forgot.

WIFE
Oh, my repentant husband!

HUSBAND
My dear soul, whom I too much have wrong'd,
For death I die, and for this have I long'd.

WIFE
Thou shouldst not—be assured—for these faults die,
If the law could forgive as soon as I.

[**CHILDREN** laid out.

HUSBAND
What sight is yonder?

WIFE
Oh, our two bleeding boys laid forth upon the threshold!

HUSBAND
Here's weight enough to make a heartstring crack!
Oh, were it lawful that your pretty souls
Might look from Heaven into your father's eyes,
Then should you see the penitent glasses melt,
And both your murthers shoot upon my cheeks!
But you are playing in the angels' laps,
And will not look on me,
Who, void of grace, kill'd you in beggary.
Oh, that I might my wishes now attain,
I should then wish you living were again,
Though I did beg with you, which thing I fear'd!
Oh, 'twas the enemy my eyes so blear'd!
Oh, would you could pray Heaven me to forgive
That will unto my end repentant live!

WIFE

It makes me e'en forget all other sorrows
And leaven part with this. Come, will you go?

HUSBAND
I'll kiss the blood I spilt and then I go:
My soul is bloodied, well may my lips be so.

[He kisses the **CHILDREN**.

Farewell, dear wife, now thou and I must part;
I of thy wrongs repent me with my heart.

WIFE
Oh, stay, thou shalt not go!

HUSBAND
That's but in vain; you must see it so.
Farewell, ye bloody ashes of my boys;
My punishments are their eternal joys.
Let every father look into my deeds,
And then their heirs may prosper while mine bleeds.

WIFE
More wretched am I now in this distress
Than former sorrows made me.

[Exeunt **HUSBAND** and **OFFICERS** guarding him with halberds.

MASTER
Oh kind wife, be comforted!
One joy is yet unmurdered:
You have a boy at nurse: your joy's in him.

WIFE
Dearer than all is my poor husband's life.
Heaven give my body strength, which yet is faint
With much expense of blood, and I will kneel,
Sue for his life, number up all my friends
To plead for pardon my dear husband's life.

MASTER
Was it in man to wound so kind a creature?
I'll ever praise a woman for thy sake.
I must return with grief, my answer's set.
I shall bring news weighs heavier than the debt:
Two brothers, one in bond lies overthrown,
This on a deadlier execution.

Thomas Middleton was born in London in April 1580 and baptised on 18th April. He was the son of a bricklayer who had raised himself to the status of a gentleman and become the owner of property adjoining the Curtain Theatre in Shoreditch.

Middleton was aged only five when his father died. His mother remarried but this new union unfortunately fell apart and turned into a fifteen year legal conflict centered on the inheritance of Thomas and his younger sister.

Middleton went on to attend Queen's College, Oxford, matriculating in 1598. However he failed to graduate for reasons unknown leaving either in 1600 or 1601. He had by that time written and published three long poems in popular Elizabethan styles. None appears to have been commercially successful although Microcynicon: Six Snarling Satirese was denounced by the Archbishop of Canterbury and publicly burned as part of his attack on verse satire. Although a minor work, the poems show the roots of Middleton's interest in, and later mature work on, sin, hypocrisy, and lust.

In the early years of the 17th century, Middleton made a living writing topical pamphlets, including one, Penniless Parliament of Threadbare Poets, that was reprinted several times as well as becoming the subject of a parliamentary inquiry.

For one so young he was already making quite an impact and had obviously attracted the eye of the authorities in those turbulent times.

Records surviving of the great theatrical entrepreneur of the day, Philip Henslowe, confirm that Middleton was writing for Henslowe's Admiral's Men. His lauded contemporary, a certain William Shakespeare, was writing only for Henslowe whereas Middleton remained a free agent and able to write for whichever theatrical company hired him.

These early years writing plays continued to attract controversy. His friendship and writing partnership with Thomas Dekker brought him into conflict with Ben Jonson and George Chapman in the so-called War of the Theatres. (This controversy was also called the Poetomachia by Thomas Dekker. The Bishops Ban of 1599 had removed any use of satire from prose and verse publications and so the only outlet was on the stage. For the next 3 years Ben Jonson and George Chapman on one side and John Marston, Thomas Dekker and Thomas Middleton on the other poked fun at their opposition with characters from their plays. The grudge against Jonson continued as late as 1626, when Jonson's play The Staple of News indulges in a slur on Middleton's last play, A Game at Chess).

In 1603, Middleton married. It was also a momentous year in other respects. On the death of Elizabeth I, her cousin James VI of Scotland was now also crowned King James I of England. Another outbreak of the plague now forced the theatres in London to close.

For Middleton the changeover from Elizabethan to Jacobean was the beginning of a long period of success as a writer.

When the theatres re-opened and welcomed back audiences in need of entertainment Middleton was there, writing for several different companies. In particular he specialised in city comedy and revenge tragedy.

During this time he appears also to have written with Shakespeare and he is variously attributed as collaborating on All's Well That Ends Well and Timon of Athens.

Although Middleton had started as a junior partner to Thomas Dekker he was now his fully fledged equal. His finest work with Dekker was undoubtedly The Roaring Girl, a biography of the notorious contemporary thief Mary Frith (Frith began her criminal career as a pickpocket before moving on to highway robbery with a penchant for dressing up as a man. A spell in prison was followed by a long career as a 'fence' from her shop in Fleet St. She lived to the then quite extraordinary age of 74.) The writing is noteworthy not only for its playwriting ambition but in producing a fully formed heroine in Moll Cutpurse. This was only shortly after the role of women in plays had seen fit to have them played, in the main, by men.

In the 1610s, Middleton began another playwriting partnership, this time with the actor William Rowley, producing another slew of plays including the classics Wit at Several Weapons and A Fair Quarrel.

The ever adaptable Middleton seemed at ease working with others or by himself. His solo writing credits include the comic masterpiece, A Chaste Maid in Cheapside, in 1613. Interestingly his solo plays are somewhat less thrusting and bellicose. Certainly there is no comedy among them with the satirical depth of Michaelmas Term and no tragedy as raw, striking and as bloodthirsty as The Revenger's Tragedy.

There may be various reasons for this and among them that he was increasingly involved with civic pageants and therefore was trying to avoid too much controversy especially without the cover of a collaborator. Indeed in 1620, he was officially appointed as chronologer of the City of London, a post he held until his death in 1627, when ironically, it passed to his great rival, and sometime enemy, Ben Jonson.

Middleton's official duties did not interrupt his dramatic writing; the 1620s saw the production of his and Rowley's tragedy, and continual favourite, The Changeling, as well as several other tragicomedies.

However in 1624, he reached a peak of notoriety when his dramatic allegory A Game at Chess was staged by the King's Men. The play used the conceit of a chess game to present and satirise the recent intrigues surrounding the Spanish Match; James I's son, Prince Charles, was being positioned to marry the daughter, Maria Anna of the Spanish King Philip IV of Spain. Though Middleton's approach was strongly patriotic, the Privy Council closed the play, after only nine performances at the Globe theatre, having received a complaint from the Spanish ambassador. The Privy Council then opened a prosecution against both authors and actors. Although Middleton in his defence showed that the play had been passed by the Master of the Revels, Sir Henry Herbert, any further performance was forbidden and the author and actors fined.

What happened next is a mystery. It is the last play recorded as having being written by Middleton. His playwriting career appears to have stopped dead. It follows that some sort of further punishment probably occurred and for a writer can there be any greater punishment than not being allowed to write or be heard?

Middleton's work is diverse even by the standards of his age. His career Middleton covers many many genres including tragedy, history and city comedy. As we have noted he did not have the kind of official relationship with a particular company that Shakespeare or Fletcher had that might have supported him in a lean creative period. Instead he appears to have written on a freelance basis for any number of companies. His output ranges from the "snarling" satire of Michaelmas Term, performed by the Children of Paul's, to the bleak intrigues of The Revenger's Tragedy, performed by the King's Men. Interestingly earlier editions of The Revenger's Tragedy attributed the play solely to Cyril Tourneur but recent studies have shredded that view so that Middleton's authorship is not now seriously contested

Indeed modern techniques in analysing writing styles are now leaning towards giving Middleton credit for his adaptation and revision of Shakespeare's Macbeth and Measure for Measure. Along with the more established evidence of collaboration on All's Well That Ends Well and Timon of Athens it appears that Middleton has moved some way forward to the front rank of playwrights and an association, in some form, but its greatest exponent.

His early work was informed by the blossoming, in the late Elizabethan period, of satire, while his maturity was influenced by the ascendancy of Fletcherian tragicomedy. Middleton's later work, in which his satirical fury is tempered and broadened, includes three of his acknowledged masterpieces. A Chaste Maid in Cheapside, produced by the Lady Elizabeth's Men, which skillfully combines London life with an expansive view of the power of love to effect reconciliation even though London seems populated entirely by sinners, in which no social rank goes unsatirised. The Changeling, a later tragedy, returns Middleton to an Italianate setting like that of The Revenger's Tragedy, except that here the central characters are more fully drawn and more compelling as individuals. Similar development can be seen in Women Beware Women.

Middleton's plays are marked by their cynicism, though often very funny, about the human race. His characters are complex. True heroes are a rarity: almost all of his characters are selfish, greedy, and self-absorbed.

When Middleton does portray good people, the characters are often presented as flawless and perfect and given small, undemanding roles. A theological pamphlet attributed to Middleton gives sustenance to the notion that Middleton was a strong believer in Calvinism.

Thomas Middleton died at his home at Newington Butts in Southwark in the summer of 1627, and was buried on July 4th, in St Mary's churchyard which today survives as a public park in Elephant and Castle.

Middleton stands with John Fletcher and Ben Jonson as the most successful and prolific of playwrights from the Jacobean period. Very few Renaissance dramatists would achieve equal success in both comedy and tragedy but Middleton was one. He also wrote many masques and pageants and remains, to this day, one of the most notable of Jacobean dramatists.

Middleton's work has long been praised by many literary critics, among the most fervent were Algernon Charles Swinburne and T. S. Eliot. The latter thought Middleton was second only to Shakespeare.

Among their contemporaries was a very crowded field of talent including: Ben Jonson (1572-1637), Christopher Marlowe (1564-1593), Francis Beaumont (1585-1616), Henry Chettle (1564-1606), John Fletcher (1579–1625), John Ford (1586–1639), John Day (1574-1640), John Marston (1576-1634), John

Webster (1580-1634), Nathan Field (1587-1620), Philip Massinger (1584-1640), Richard Burbage (1567-1619), Robert Greene (1558-1592), Thomas Dekker (1575-1625), Thomas Kyd (1558-1594), William Haughton (died 1605), William Rowley (1585-1626).

It's a daunting list and confirms that to top that made you a very special talent indeed.

Thomas Middleton – A Concise Bibliography

It has long been recognised that the modern concept of authorship was rather more elastic in centuries past. Writers were not only for hire, and their work therefore a commodity, but their plays ran much shorter lengths; two weeks being a common term of performance. To that themes and scenes were liberally excised from one play and used in another. Revisions to past plays that were being restaged would be undertaken and entirely credited to other writers. Many works and plays were unpublished and have not survived and some only from memory by actors etc. Whilst many of these playwrights are only now feted for their talents, some undoubtedly were at the time, but it is difficult to, in every case, to establish exact provenance. With modern scholarly and literary techniques author attributions have sometimes changed or been re-balanced. For those where this may be the case we have placed the *Play's Title and other information* in italics

Plays
Blurt, Master Constable or The Spaniard's Night Walk (with Thomas Dekker (1602)
The Phoenix (1603–4)
The Honest Whore, Part 1, a city comedy (1604), (with Thomas Dekker)
Michaelmas Term, a city comedy, (1604)
All's Well That Ends Well (1604-5); believed by some to be co-written by Middleton based on stylometric analysis.
A Trick to Catch the Old One, a city comedy (1605)
A Mad World, My Masters, a city comedy (1605)
A Yorkshire Tragedy, a one-act tragedy (1605); attributed to Shakespeare on its title page, but stylistic analysis favours Middleton.
Timon of Athens a tragedy (1605–6); stylistic analysis indicates that Middleton may have written this play in collaboration with William Shakespeare.
The Puritan (1606)
The Revenger's Tragedy (1606). Earlier editions often mistakenly attribute authorship to Cyril Tourneur.
Your Five Gallants, a city comedy (1607)
The Family of Love (1607) some attribute this to Middleton others include Dekker and Lording Barry.
The Bloody Banquet (1608–9); co-written with Thomas Dekker.
The Roaring Girl, a city comedy depicting the exploits of Mary Frith (1611); with Thomas Dekker.
No Wit, No Help Like a Woman's, a tragic-comedy (1611)
The Second Maiden's Tragedy, a tragedy (1611); an anonymous manuscript; stylistic analysis indicates Middleton's authorship (though one scholar also attributed it to Shakespeare).
A Chaste Maid in Cheapside, a city comedy (1613)
Wit at Several Weapons, a city comedy (1613); printed as part of the Beaumont and Fletcher Folio, but stylistic analysis indicates comprehensive revision by Middleton & Rowley.
More Dissemblers Besides Women, a tragicomedy (1614)

The Widow (1615–16)

The Witch, a tragicomedy (1616)

A Fair Quarrel, a tragicomedy (1616). Co-written with William Rowley.

The Old Law, a tragicomedy (1618–19). written with William Rowley and perhaps a third collaborator.

Hengist, King of Kent, or The Mayor of Quinborough, a tragedy (1620)

Women Beware Women, a tragedy (1621)

Measure for Measure (1603-4); some scholars argue that the First Folio text was partly revised by Middleton in 1621.

Anything for a Quiet Life, a city comedy (1621). Co-written with John Webster.

The Changeling, a tragedy (1622). Co-written with William Rowley.

The Nice Valour (1622). Printed as part of the Beaumont and Fletcher Folio, but stylistic analysis indicates comprehensive revision by Middleton.

The Spanish Gypsy, a tragicomedy (1623). Believed to be a play by Middleton & Rowley and later revised by Thomas Dekker and John Ford.

A Game at Chess, a political satire (1624). Satirized the negotiations over the proposed marriage of Prince Charles, son of James I of England, with the Spanish princess. Closed after nine performances.

Masques & Entertainments

The Whole Royal and Magnificent Entertainment Given to King James Through the City of London (1603–4). Co-written with Thomas Dekker, Stephen Harrison & Ben Jonson.

The Manner of his Lordship's Entertainment

The Triumphs of Truth

Civitas Amor

The Triumphs of Honour and Industry (1617)

The Masque of Heroes, or, The Inner Temple Masque (1619)

The Triumphs of Love and Antiquity (1619)

The World Tossed at Tennis (1620). Co-written with William Rowley.

Honourable Entertainments (1620–1)

An Invention (1622)

The Sun in Aries (1621)

The Triumphs of Honour and Virtue (1622)

The Triumphs of Integrity with The Triumphs of the Golden Fleece (1623)

The Triumphs of Health and Prosperity (1626)

Poetry

The Wisdom of Solomon Paraphrased (1597)

Microcynicon: Six Snarling Satires (1599)

The Ghost of Lucrece (1600)

Burbage epitaph (1619)

Bolles epitaph (1621)

Duchess of Malfi (commendatory poem) (1623)

St James (1623)

To the King (1624)

Prose

The Penniless Parliament of Threadbare Poets (1601)
News from Gravesend. Co-written with Thomas Dekker (1603)
The Nightingale and the Ant aka Father Hubbard's Tales (1604)
The Meeting of Gallants at an Ordinary (1604). Co-written with Thomas Dekker.
Plato's Cap Cast at the Year 1604 (1604)
The Black Book (1604)
Sir Robert Sherley his Entertainment in Cracovia (1609) (translation).
The Two Gates of Salvation (1609), or The Marriage of the Old and New Testament.
The Owl's Almanac (1618)
The Peacemaker (1618)